LEARNING TO SPEAK
KAT SAVAGE

UNDERWATER MOUNTAINS PUBLISHING
LOS ANGELES, CALIFORNIA
A SECRET COMPANY

LEARNING TO SPEAK BY KAT SAVAGE
EDITED AND ARRANGED BY HARRISON GORMAN
COVER AND INTERIOR ART BY KAT SAVAGE

COPYRIGHT 2015 © UNDERWATER MOUNTAINS PUBLISHING
WWW.UNDERWATERMOUNTAINS.COM

ACKNOWLEDGEMENTS

For my parents, Kim & Scott — Thank you for believing in me, for shaping me, and for letting me make mistakes. I love you dearly, and I hope I made you proud.

For my children, Kali & Kaden — Mommy is trying. I love you more than you will ever know. This is all for you.

For my sisters, Angela, Caroline, Gabrielle & Brittany — You will never know the profound affect you have had on my life. We are all in different places, but please know I love you. I only ever wanted to be a big sister you could be proud of.

For Eli — Thank you for everything you have done, everything you are doing, and everything you will do.

For Jarod — You saw this as a reality long before I ever dreamed it alive. Thank you for believing in me when I didn't. Thank you for being the best thing to happen to me in a very long time. I hope to keep you. I boob you.

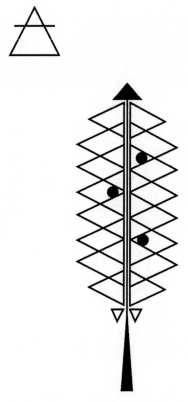

PRE-VERBAL PHASE
when we used hieroglyphs and sign language

BODY LANGUAGE

These men stare at me.
They lick their lips and
blow me kisses.
They send winks my way,
and I don't know how
to flirt back.

I am a 13-year-old girl,
and my body deceives
these men.
It is draped in
womanly camouflage.
My curves are
beyond my years.
My breasts are full
and distract from
my childhood heart
buried beneath them.

Society would later tell me
their looks, their attention
means that I am beautiful,
that I am desirable.

I don't know how to feel.
No one told me how to
use my body yet.
I will either disappoint them
or myself.

HOPE

She is 4 years old.
Her father calls her beautiful, buys her princess dresses,
and makes his way into her bedroom too late at night.

She is 13 years old.
A boy touches her developing breasts on the school bus,
but he also called her pretty, so she doesn't want to tell anyone.

She is 17 years old.
He takes her innocence, or what's left of it,
under an unremarkable night sky on the bench seat
of his truck, and he calls it love.

She is 22 years old.
He feeds her another shot of cheap liquor at a college party
and tells her he will walk her home.
She finds herself gathering her clothes from his floor
the next morning and leaves amidst his silence.

She is 29 years old.
She says yes because no one ever taught her
that saying no was okay.
She thinks sex is as close to love as she can get—
like if he wants her body, it must be because he cares about her soul.

She is 31 years old.
He holds her hand and kisses her goodnight.
She invites him in and he tells her that wasn't the reason
he came. She smiles and sees in him something
she had long forgotten to keep searching for.

THE RAPE POEM

This room smells like ass, and when I say it smells like ass,
I really mean it smells like sex.
This room smells like fucking, like dried up sweat glands,
like latex condoms, like maybe everybody had a good time.

There is a girl sitting on the floor.
She is crying to herself, careful not to wake him.

Him. Still asleep. Naked, under the sheets.

Him. He. The boy. The boy who held her the night before,
amidst beer bottles and cigarette smoke, the boy who pulled
her closer, pulled her in.

Into his arms. Into his room. Into his bed.

She never said yes. She never said no.
She was just there.

And silence is not synonymous with consent.

This room smells like rape.
This room smells like a tomb.
This room smells like one more.

A LITTLE DEATH

He birthed hell in my flesh,
touching it while a tiny voice
screaming "No!"
was trapped beneath defiled
layers of skin.

The next few years were filled
with more foreign hands,
more foreign sex.
And the screams inside all
sounded the same
until they didn't sound like
anything at all.

My body was not my own,
and even though
I stopped the hemorrhaging,
sunrise is always going to feel
a little bit like death,
and my skin is always
going to burn.

WHAT THEY WANTED

You told me I was good in bed,
fucking great in fact.
You told me I was good in bed,
but I already knew that.

I had spent years since the loss
of my virginity attempting to perfect everything
men love.
I learned what to do with my hands,
with my mouth,
with my body,
how to please the men who wanted
me to please them.

You told me I was good in bed,
and I told you
I just wanted to be good at
the only thing
men ever wanted me for.

UNBLOOMED

We fucked without rubbers,
dumping tiny seeds in my belly
that would never bloom.

I lost my softness to you.
I was nothing more than coal
and sea foam.

I am an undead garden
with no revival in sight.

TRAIN WRECK

I was good enough to look at
but not good enough to touch.

I was good enough to look at
but not good enough to touch.

I am a train wreck you pass
impossibly slowly.
You're unable to look away from my
bellowing black smoke and
my shrapnel flying through the air
like startled birds
and home run baseballs.

In so many ways
you think I am beautiful,
and in so many ways
you are relieved to be
at a safe distance.

You cannot look away
from my magnificence,
but you are so glad
you are not mangled
in my steel.

WHEN YOU BECOME WHAT THEY HAVE MADE YOU

These men were not kind to me.
They used me and disposed of me
like a dull razor or a styrofoam cup.

They took what they wanted from me
and threw the rest away.
Some sooner than others,
but the throwing away is
always inevitable.

And somehow I am the one
standing here apologizing.

I'm trying to remember
what I was before I felt worthless
and why I thought I'd find love
behind the open zippers
of their pants.

My happiness was laced
around their fingertips,
laced around my neck.
After swimming an ocean
of memories,
I'm coming up empty at
the exact moment
I branded myself so unlovable.

Attempting to move beyond this
feels like I'm running through
a house of mirrors searching for
the exit and growing dizzy
from my reflection.

FIXER

I'm standing here with my mouth open,
panting like a dog, and it's a little pathetic,
but I have always been this way.

I am a fixer.

I see you limping over regret and trying to
gather enough strength to choke down each mistake,
each thing that left you a little more injured with every move.

I can fix it.

I see you there replacing bandages over old memories
and trying on prosthetics with the hope that the
ghost limbs that linger will dissipate.

Let me fix it.

Here I am playing nurse, playing surgeon.
I say things to you like,
"Let me lick your wounds clean. I can make you forget."

I am a fixer.

This has never been a successful practice,
there has never been smooth post-op recovery.
I have lost them all on the table or soon after.
Still I am here, attempting to fix in you
what will never really heal.

I can fix it.

You let me pull your skin tight—
thinking I can hold it together for you,
knowing my hands will
give way long before your pain, but
serving as a welcomed distraction.

I thought I could fix you.

LIKE PILLOWS

We crashed into each other.
No.
Do not think of a car accident.
It was not violent.
We did not hurt anyone.

Think instead of two pillows
gliding toward each other in slow motion,
yielding to one another,
folding around each other,
and releasing flightless feathers
into the air.

When they fell to the floor,
they were still tucked together
as if they were one.

We crashed like pillows.
Softly. Beautifully.
We didn't make a sound.

CONVERSATIONS WITH ACCEPTANCE

"I want to curl up inside your heart
and rest inside your mind," he said.

"What if my heart is an abandoned house
where the windows are all boarded up?
What if there is no rest in my mind?
What if there's a hurricane inside?" I replied.

"If there is love in a home, it is a palace
for sure," he quoted Tom Waits.
"And as for the wind, it's fine for flying kites,
and I like kites," he answered.

I hope when he climbs inside, he wants
to stay, despite this disheveled house and
the constant zephyr coming in under the door.

I think this is what it feels like
to have someone to accept you as you are.

ЯΔTH

I measured the space in the room between us
like I was dissecting angles in a 10th grade geometry class—
thinking if I solved for X,
where X represents the distance between the palms
of our outstretched hands reaching for each other,
then there'd be no reason to ask Y,
only Y not?

SOME KIND OF WAY

The only thing I've ever been sure of
in my entire miserable existence
is that I was meant to love you.

I don't know for how long
or even in what way.

I just know it's written in the lines
on the palms of my hands.

So take hold of them.
Take hold of me.

LOVESICK

Drench me in white orchids
and all of your maybes
until my skin is a reflection
of all the possibilities
hidden in your suitcase.

I'm throwing up shy smiles,
lovesick all over the sidewalk
and hoping we can wander home
together.

WANTING

I want to hold him,
and I want to kiss him.
I want to touch him
with daisy fingertips
and tell him all the things
I stopped myself from saying
every time he'd walked past me
for the last six months.
I want to ask him what his
middle name is
and find out what kind of
shampoo he likes.
I rehearsed scenarios
in my mind about what
finally saying hello to him
might be like,
but I could never bring myself to follow through,
to really try to begin something with him.
To even speak the word beginning
suggests the coming of an end.
There doesn't have to be
any endings in my daydreams,
so I'm keeping him there
just a little while longer.

CANARY MEMORIES

My lungs are brown paper bags,
and I can hear them fold in
on themselves every time I lose
my breath to the memory of
the first time you kissed me.
And I know,
sooner or later, they're going to
catch fire and leave soot
smeared across my birdcage ribs.

SEASONS

Wrap me in your summer glow
and we'll spend sunsets
speaking in a foreign tongue.

We can make our own
fireworks in July while
lying on a blanket somewhere
in the middle of nowhere.

We'll take to the water
in August to keep cool
and stay calm.

As September comes to an end,
I'll try to keep my eyes from leaking.

Don't worry,
I won't ask you where
you spend your winters.

IN THE MIDDLE

I'm not good at this.
I'm never going to be good at this.
This thing that isn't exactly love
and isn't exactly friendship either.
It's messy here in the middle—
unsure of which way to turn,
carrying buckets full of wasted emotion
that you don't want and that
I can't reuse.
They're getting so heavy.
I don't know how to navigate here.
My compass just keeps spinning,
and my map blew away in the wind.
I don't know how to get from here
to somewhere that doesn't hurt
when you tell me
"Not tonight."

REARRANGED

You split me open down my left side
from temple to hip bone,
rearranged my vital organs in your image,
shoved it all back in, stitched me up,
and smiled at your creation.

I wasn't born to worship you.
You broke in, with the help of
your X-Acto knife guile,
and you made me this way.

SEWN

I'm having trouble finding my feet.
I have forgotten how to run from
the things that are bad for me,
and you take advantage of my
cloudy knees and silent lips.
Open your eyelids.
I think you can see how damaged
my ability to love is,
yet
I find you carelessly reaping the rewards
of what so many others before you
have sewn clumsily into my skin
with thick crimson thread
and needles of hope.

UNKEPT WORDS

I'm starting to think you talk to everyone else
exactly as you talk to me;
there's nothing coming from your mouth to call my own.
So all the pretty things from my mouth
that were once branded just for you,
I'm starting to share with everyone too.
I was lying to all of those people
to keep myself from telling you the truth.

PHONE LINES

Did you feel that?
Tectonic plates shifted
and, as you smiled across the phone lines,
the air got so thick in the space between us,
it felt as if it collapsed on itself and you were
no more than a few steps away with
arms outstretched and ready to wrap around me
the same way the phone lines do
when I've started to miss the feeling of you.

REARVIEW MIRROR HABITS

I was checking my rearview mirror
because you pulled out of the parking lot
directly behind me,
and I just keep checking to make sure
you haven't floated into another lane
or another dream.

We used to kiss sometimes
and meet for breakfast too.
I'm looking back to see if you're smiling
and possibly reminiscing.
I was always just hoping you weren't
trying to forget.

I was waiting for a crack in your face,
for a smile to break though.
I was looking so intently into my
rearview
that I couldn't see the brake lights
flooding the road ahead.

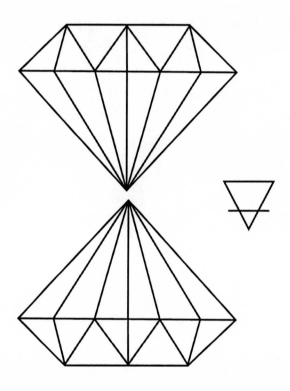

ARTICULATION DISORDER

and all the words are just noise

ƉIGGINC ƉEEPER

You are asleep beside me.

I place stones in my pockets
to sink down to wherever your mind is.

You feel so far away all the time
and even further when we are both sleeping.

I reach out to touch your shoulder,
but my fingers curl into my palm
before we connect.

I cradle myself instead.

Moments later, I find myself outside
under a starless sky,
digging for more stones,
digging them up like they might save us.

TIN CUP WORDS

You wrote things I thought only existed in fake love letters
and in movies between fake people,
but they were lies too sweet not to believe.

I buried them in the backyard like my favorite bone
or a time capsule so I could dig them up later,
resurrect them under a different moon,
and remember what it felt like to be a goddess
adorned with a crown of thorns and false promises.

Your next lover will wonder why you have no words for her,
why you can't put together any beautiful verses for her,
why your voice scratches when you speak like a robot, like sandpaper,
like a broken record, like someone who ran out
of things to say to people they think they care about.

When she asks you why, tell her you've reached your limit,
tell her the last words you gave are hidden under a pile of dirt,
tell her they're not worth anything anyway.
Let her know they make up nothing more than a tin cup
painted in gold flakes.
The paint will start to rub off on her hands, and you will leave her there—
holding nothing but an empty, rusted cup,
panhandling for words like the beggars beg for spare change.

VIOLENT GOODBYE

You carved your name
in my gums
because I foolishly let you
sleep inside my mouth—
all wet and glossy,
reflecting your
hazel lies.

I woke up the next morning
to a dead tongue
and the white-chalked outline
of your violent goodbye.

WHAT WE FORGET

You were a forced concept,
and all the other things
I hated about myself.
I was here,
choking on polluted dreams
and praying for salvation
I was no longer sure existed in you.
Neither of us were going to wake up
suddenly happy
behind a metaphoric
white picket fence,
and I was becoming
increasingly aware of my
itching feet
stepping slowly
toward an exit sign.
My lungs were lusting
for new oxygen
while my heart sat idle—
it had forgotten to want
anything
more than this.

WITHOUT FIRE

I close my eyes.
I press my ear against the bare skin
of your chest like I would with a conch shell,
expecting to hear the ocean.

I can't hear anything, and I don't know
whether that's my fault or yours.

Where is the pounding of your heart?
Where is the magic inside you?

I open my eyes.
Tears are running down my face
because I don't know how long
you have been hollow,
without movement in your belly.

DISSIMILARITY

Did she crack open your chest yet?

Did she split you down the middle and crawl inside?

Did she try to build a home with your bones?

All I wanted to do was hold your hand.

LIQUID RECOLLECTION

Even on nights like tonight,
when drinks are flowing
and friendly laughs fill the air,
you're still right at the edge
of my thoughts,
begging for attention.
And after enough liquor,
I can't help but give in
and swim through an
ocean of memories
to find you waiting
on my cognitive shore.

WHAT YOU AWAKEN

You don't understand what you have awoken within me,
and I'm sure you have no intention to cultivate it.
You split open old wounds
and—through scar tissue—made your way
to the cynicism carved in my bones as if on
whittled wood or a marble headstone.
You made them soft like marshmallows
with pretty words and blank gestures.
You sparked your Zippo against your leg
like the cool guys do in the movies,
and I was so lost in the motion
I didn't notice you were tossing it at
my gasoline feet.
You burned all the good in me to the ground.
You weren't supposed to expose a woman like that.
You weren't supposed to awaken her love
and leave her as a scorched relic.

PHONE CALL

When you call me on the telephone,
I'm afraid you can hear me holding my breath
with my eyes wide open.

I'm afraid you can hear me waiting.

There's an echo coming through the phone line,
and I'm saying everything twice
but you can't hear my voice.

You can hear anything
except the parts of me making noise.

BRUISED

My bruised belly matches my bruised ego,
and you will never know how sorry I am
that my mind is a dried up lake—
a vapid wasteland filled with broken parts
and spare wishes.
I am cloaked in a questionable past,
and there is no room for anything else.
Not even you.

LOST

The clock ticks
and the sun sets
and the moon rises.

Where am I?

I don't hear any birds.
There is a train coming.
The weatherman says
it's supposed to be nice tomorrow.

Where am I?

I think my sister wants to see me
for lunch.
There is a bottle growing emptier.
I'm almost out of smokes.

Where am I?

All the while I sit here,
missing the parts of me
I lost to you.

BLOOD SPATTER NORTH

I can no longer tell whether you are the expelled bullet
or the smoking barrel.

Either way, I'm standing here with a hole in my chest,
and anything I had of worth within me is now spattered
on the wall behind me.

And you, my dear,
you carry indifference in your hands so well
like a gun;
I realize now you may have been taking aim
the entire time.

CATCH AND RELEASE

You do things that tug at me.
There are all these invisible little strings
attached to every important thing I know,
and every now and then
you give them a little yank
and then retreat as if it was an accident.
You say,
"Oh no, no. I didn't mean that."

So I float back away.
Another tug,
and we repeat.

Your apologies sound like atom bombs
punctuated with question marks.

Why did you ever tug?
Please, cut the strings.

PALM READING

I thought my hand fit perfectly in yours,
and I thought maybe that was a sign,
like maybe we were meant to be.
I don't know why it took me so long
to see that I had been holding my own
hand this entire time.
This entire time, I had been carrying
the weight of us on my own.
My arms are tired.
I look down at my palms.
They ache,
and you are nowhere
on my lifeline.

FULL IS A MAGIC TRICK

I kept filling you up,
molding all the
best parts of me
to fit in your empty spaces,
until there was nothing left
but the smoke and mirrors
you'd set up
to make me believe
I was still full enough
to keep filling you.

WE ARE ALL JUST SILLY

Silly boy.
You wanted to unclench my thighs,
unravel me, and see what was at my center.

Silly boy.
You didn't know you were
unraveling such a mess.
I thought it only fair to show you
my warning labels and let you
decide for yourself.

Silly girl.
Here I thought he might stay.

SUCKER PUNCH

You filled my hollow bones
with false promises
and cigarette butts
and a little bit of the Pacific.

And you didn't understand
why it was so hard for me to
let you go.

The morning after you left,
I found your toothbrush still resting neatly
next to mine.

I wipe the blood from my mouth.

Goddammit,
you got me good.

SECRET KEEPING MOON

I just need you to hold me
long enough for me to fall asleep.

And then you can slink back across the room
as if it never happened.

I promise the moon
will keep your secret.

AT HIM

I write poems at him rather than about him.
I write them like I expect an answer.
I write them like he'll argue back.
I write poems at him,
like whispering into his ear at night, or
like screaming across all the distance between us.
I write poems at him like he's still here,
like he isn't completely gone,
like he still has a voice here with me.

BEND/BREAK

I just wanted you to bend a little,
wanted to create a soft curve in you,
shove aside your organs
and make space to resemble the crescent
shape of the moon—
something I could fit comfortably into.

If you could just bend a little,
maybe I could fit
without having to break.
I wouldn't have to walk away.

JUMPING

Sometimes happiness comes along.
But in my experience,
it always leaves too.
Sometimes the leaving is quick—
a camera flashes, then you're
staring at a different picture
than you were before. Overexposure.
Sometimes the leaving is slow.
The distance subtly grows
between lovers over the course
of too many quiet meals.
I'm still trying to figure out
which form of hurt I prefer.
It's like choosing between
the jump
and
the descent.

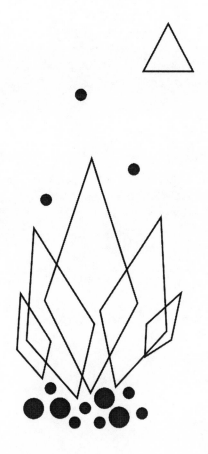

DISSECTING THE TONGUE
trying to fix the stutter

HALF-LOVERS

It's ok. I will be fine.
I have survived this too many times.
Though I have to wonder how many times
I can blow my own leg off before it is
no longer a leg and can never be a leg again.
These not-quite, very-nearly lovers
half-hold me for a moment.
They cannot lose me,
do not want all of me,
and I don't know how to break myself down
into something fractional for them.
These half-lovers—the almost, just-shy-of lovers—they never stay long.
They stay too long.

VIDEO GAMES

You played me like a video game.
Every move I made, I made under your control.
I fought for you over and over again
and died too many times
until you decided not to continue,
to play another round.

STOCKHOLM SYNDROME

He tells me plainly that he is void of goodness,
but all I can see is the good in him.
He tells me he has hurt people,
and I tell him we have all hurt people.
He tells me he will end up hurting me,
and I tell him that it's okay.
Is this the part where someone tells me
that I am the victim who has
fallen in love with her captor?

GIVE ME A LIE

Hold me just a moment longer
like everything is fine
and nothing is changing.

Before you leave,
hold me just a moment longer
and make *goodbye* feel like
see you later
one last time.

It's the least you can do.

RECLAIMED PARTS

You reached in slow, passed jagged broken teeth and
down my gullet, searching for the half-bitten fruit
you once gifted me.
You cut away from my flesh the love
you had planted there with kisses and sweat.
You clipped each feather from my bruised wings,
the ones that had taken me so long to earn.
You built me up delicately
only to reclaim everything but the foundation.
I've got nothing left but bones,
and I'm pretty sure those were borrowed.

YOUR MOUTH

You let me kiss it,
run my fingertips over it,
listen to it tell me everything
and nothing I'd ever wanted
to hear.
I had always been captivated
with the way the edge of it
curled up in amusement
or straightened out when
your eyes grew dark.
Lately there has been
no curve to it,
no laughing,
nothing vibrant.
I once was caught in something
dreamlike,
something induced by
Ambien and merlot.
I caught you leaving
out of the corner of my eye,
hazy and slate-colored.
I watched you leave your
mouth behind—
like you didn't need it anymore,
like you could just get a new one,
like everything it had collected
from me was
easy to abandon.

ME, THE SINKING SHIP

The weight of it,
the immense weight of it,
clung to my skin
like dirt under my fingernails,
and I was no longer sure
I knew how to continue on
carrying it while sweat
rolled down my neck.
There were little bits
of my spirit escaping me
in the form of a sinking ship.

GENTLE PAIN

I didn't want to compare you to anything ugly
or depressing.
The absence of your love wasn't unbearable.
It was kind of like the feeling that comes
after blowing out a birthday candle
or watching a pebble make ripples on a glassy pond.
That's why I think it hurts so much.
The party is over,
and the ripples have been silenced
on the edge of the shore.
The beauty I once absorbed from these moments,
from our love,
is all gone.
It went quietly,
and that leads to the worst kind of pain.

FINDING YOUR VOICE

I've crawled inside a broken clock,
and I'm climbing between the cogs
just to find where the noise has gone.
The quiet is whispering to me,
and I miss your voice
like the dead language I hear
in yesterday's dreams.
It sounds nothing like a lullaby
and everything like an addiction
I've found myself missing.

SHABBY CONSTRUCTION

I remember when you embraced me
like maybe I was the only thing
that mattered,
and maybe I was in that moment.
Perfect moments have a way of
dissipating,
crumbling to make room for cold truths.
Now you hold her the same way
you once held me.
And now I realize
your bones aren't built for devotion.

WAITING

I lay there waiting.
I was always just waiting
as I slowly rotted,
sinking into quicksand.

Loose teeth.
Bleeding gums.

Blackened edges faded
into a sky without stars.

And I don't know
where the moon went.

It was so cold,
and sunrise
was so far away.

OUT OF PRAYERS

I look like all the failure I have ever felt.

And I don't know when I learned
to be the woman who wants
the people who don't want her.

My knees are rubber bands.
My teeth are tiny stones.

I blame you for the constellations
I can no longer recognize,
and all I ever did was love you
like a woman
who had run out of prayers.

MUSEUM OF HEARTS

I know somewhere
you have my heart in an exhibit,
with pins holding it open on display
in one of those cases that usually keep
beautiful dead butterflies.
I know you like to watch as it
struggles through the agony—
still trying to beat for you
in all its reckless glory.

TACKLING VICES

There are little white pills on my bedside table
mumbling promises of peace,
and I have a genetic predisposition
to addiction.
It was only a matter of time really
before something took hold of me.
I just hadn't stumbled across it yet.
I thought maybe I had once, though.
He was tall and smelled like rain.
His hands were twice mine,
but his touch wasn't fierce.
And in my entire life,
I don't think I've ever lost myself
to anything quite like that.
I rethought what it meant to be
addicted,
and it tasted a lot like being in love.
There are little white pills on my bedside table
sitting next to a phone
with his name on the screen,
and I just need him to answer.

QUIET FIRE

We started to cough heavily
and our eyes started to water,
but we just kept on walking.

We stopped talking about the future
like it was a destination
we were meant to arrive at together.

We saw it instead as a
fluorescent exit sign
in the dark hallway of
a burning building.

And we had been deaf to
the smoke alarms.

NEAR-DEATH EXPERIENCE

I like to believe you still think of me
even when her lips are pressed hard
against yours,
like the near-death experience
you can't stop reliving in your head.
Even now,
when your life is seemingly perfect.

Tell me,
can she taste the shadow of death
on your tongue?

THE REAPER'S SONG

There are small birds
nesting in my throat
amongst rusty words
and dying lilacs, which line
the rest of my insides.
They peck around
until pinholes appear.
They chirp in a another language.

Can you hear it?
Or are you too far away now?

You left the door unlocked.
Can you hear it?

It's the reaper's song.

IT'S TOO LOUD

I hear your name
echoing in my veins.
And sometimes it
sounds like muffled waves,
and sometimes it's
a violent wake,
but always it's
too loud to ignore.

I pick up the phone
to call you as if I've
forgotten you'd
told me to stop.

You will not pick up
and the empty air over the line
reminds me I am alone.

ABANDONED

My heart is an abandoned house,
with the windows boarded up
and the front doorknob missing.

People came to visit,
they came and went,
left their garbage,
left anything they no longer wanted.

There are ghosts in the walls
and regret has been ground into
the carpet.

No one wants to live here.
Not even me.

NO SHADOW GRAVEYARD

I've got the ghost of who I thought you were
tucked inside my invisible breast pocket,
and sometimes it's cold against my skin
like the first snowflakes of the first snowfall
in the first winter after too many consecutive summers.
Sometimes it burns until my flesh is smoking
and my freckles are
snap   crackle   pop
like firecrackers or your smile.
I don't know how to let go of who you never were.
There are no graveyards for shadows.

OUCH

Saltwater and goodbye kisses.

A new shade of lipstick
for my wounded mouth.

All my lovers tell me
I taste like agony and tobacco.

They want to know what happened to me
and who marked me worthless.

I say your name
and spit out rusted nails
as I try to throw up what's left of you.

I'm not going to pretend it doesn't hurt
when I try.

DEAD IN THE MIDDLE

My skeleton is gone.
It'd been ripped out from the bottom of my feet
and hung like a decoration above a mantle,
leaving me with a mound of soft flesh
and no femurs or tibias to carry me away.
Maybe I could move if I had at least been left
a backbone.
Reconstruct me and put my skull
in the pit of my stomach,
fill my head with helium
and leave the rest at the roadside memorial—
caked in dried blood
between the pause and the punchline,
between the *when* and the *if*,
between now and yesterday.

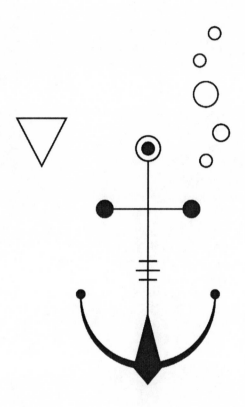

ℂOMMUNICATION ℝEMEDIATION

this is a language intervention

HOW IT FEELS

Some days it won't matter,
and it won't feel cold,
and he will be far away from your mind.

Some days it will be a siren;
it will be heavy in the pit of your stomach.
On those days, you'll have to take shelter.

If it helps, the space between the hard days will grow,
but most days, it'll feel like your keychain is too heavy.

PENNY MOUTH

My mouth tastes like pennies
but I don't remember giving him change.

I remember
in slow motion
the sight of him walking into the kitchen,
drinking a glass of water,
and gathering his shoes from the edge of my bed.

I don't remember watching him leave,
only the sound of the door.
Swoosh, swing, shut—bang.

I spit pennies out into the bathroom sink—
clink clink—
but they look a lot like drops of blood.

I lie down in clean bed sheets and shut my eyes.

Tomorrow I will not love him.

SELF-PRESERVATION

Throw out all the bath towels he ever used
and buy new soap—
the old kind will always smell like him.

Pile too many pillows on the empty side of the
bed, which you should also wrap in new linens.

Stop watching the shows you watched together
and refrain from going to that bar down the street.

Unframe the photographs,
delete phone numbers,
and let him keep the kitchen table
so you can't miss him sitting across from you.

You cannot unmeet him,
but you can unknow him.

This is not getting over him.

This is what self-preservation looks like.

SOLE OR SOUL

I am running.
I can feel pangs of heat
in the muscles of my tired legs
and I'm almost breathless
as my chest rises and falls,
attempting to keep up with my mind.

I am running circles around houses
and street lamps in the pursuit of something,
in the pursuit of nothing.

I am running, and all I can hear
is the pitter-pat of
sole smashing against pavement,
hoping something shakes out.

10 STEPS TO SOMEWHERE BETTER

1
I thought I knew you better than I knew myself.

2
There's a mockingbird outside my window, and I think she's
making fun of me.

3
I'm gathering up the leftover scraps of our relationship
to make a patchwork quilt for your bed.

4
The mockingbird is laughing, and it resembles your laugh or maybe mine.

5
I keep pricking my fingers with these needles, and
the thread is knotted up like my stomach.

6
The mockingbird is flapping its wings and throwing its head back
in a display of confidence, which I lack.

7
I'm sorry if parts of this quilt are tear-stained, but I remember
how much you liked my pillowcases, so I cut them up and sewed them in.

8
I think the mockingbird has been crying this whole time, and
I can't be sure, but I think she wants to be more than a reflection
in the window.

9
Your quilt is all done but I can't bring myself to hand it over to you knowing that
it will drape over a bed that no longer holds us but instead
holds piles of ash and good intentions.

10
The mockingbird falls over on its side, and I watch her give her last breath as
she watches her reflection take flight—sometimes dying is necessary in order to
let the best parts of you live on.

NON-SELECTIVE FEELING

At the end of the day,
when all the dirt and blood
is wiped away from the wounds
that will soon blister over
to join my collection of scars,
I can't help but breathe easy
knowing I'd rather feel
everything
than nothing at all.

LEARNING TO WALK AGAIN

I walk with heavy feet
as though the weight of all
the heartache and pain
I have collected has been drained
into the flats of them,
and maybe if I threw them
against the pavement hard enough,
all that pain would explode
from the tips of my toes—
leaving minimal damage,
leaving me almost whole.
I could learn to walk proudly once again,
with steps light like feathers,
graceful like a dancer's feet,
like anything that had never appeared to hurt.

THE FRUIT

You twist and turn underneath an orange sky—
glinting, glistening like diamonds or broken glass.
I watch you peel an apple, cut it in half,
expose the seeds, and then discard them.
I watch you do this to a plum next,
and then a pear after that.
You take a bite from each, searching.
The orange sky turns purple, and you
give up for today.
You say you will try again tomorrow.
This is when you return to me;
you have always been the blade,
and I have always been your sharpening stone.
You would be so dull without me,
and your edge cannot make easy work of me
like it could the fruit and the seeds and the fruitless trees.

INSTEAD OF NUMB

I wake up from a thick night
filled with longing palpitations and a
cold sweat that has something to do
with the pangs in my bloodstream.

Somehow these bits of discomfort
console me.

Without them,
I would be numb.

NECESSARY HEMORRHAGE

Healing is the most ridiculous concept I have ever tried to wrap my mind around.

Google defines healing as the act or process of becoming sound or healthy again.

Almost as if to imply that what has happened can unhappen, as if to imply that we can take what has happened to us, slap a Band-Aid over it, and in a week or so, we'll be just fine.

I'm calling bullshit.

Tell me to bandage my fractured ribs where I inhaled him too fast and exhaled him too long, and tell me I will heal with just a little time and ointment.

Tell me I can suture my splitting tongue, one half searching for the taste of his name, the other longing to spit him out.

Tell me I will be rid of this fever, the kind that has be bedridden.

Tell me I can take a pill and sleep him off.

I have a feeling it can't be done.

At the very least, do not tell me I will heal if you cannot provide a remedy for what ails me.

Do not pretend you are the surgeon that can remove him from me and stitch me shut.

Just let me lie here and bleed him out like bad blood. It will be over soon.

NOT MEANT TO BE

I couldn't shake the feeling that, all this time,
I simply didn't satisfy your soul.
You found me lacking whatever it was you needed,
whatever it was you craved.

Try as I may have,
I would never be able to change that.

We weren't meant to re-write stories
or rearrange stars.

The best I can do now is let you go.
Gently. Easily. Peacefully.

Even if it means I have to grieve,
at least you'll have a chance at happiness.

WHAT REMAINS

I miss you.
And,
if I could,
I would stop.
There is
no process
for forgetting.
At best,
I can push
you far away
and let
the rays of the sun
fade you
over time.
Your bones,
however,
would
always
remain.

THE SUN

I'm sitting outside in my backyard,
and it's such a beautiful day.
Warm light licks my exposed skin,
and I should be happy.

I think I will be happy
one day if that's any consolation.

The sun is really good at things like
spurring photosynthesis,
drying tears,
bringing tomorrow.

PICKING SIDES

All this time later—
through all these sleepless nights,
through all the worry,
and all the countless conversations
turned red by the absence of conviction
in our fruitless throats—
there was only one question
for me to ask myself:

Did I want to be the bloody lip
or the bloody knuckles?

BURY IT

You are my favorite memory,
all violet and throes.

I hold onto it
as tightly as I can with these
bruised hands, but lately
I don't know why.

I crack open my collection of memories,
the ones tagged with your name,
on days I want to laugh and cry
at the same time,
on days I need to feel too much
all at once,
on days I want to stop myself
from crossing the silence
to get to you.

You are my favorite memory,
but I need to bury you in the back now.

NOTHING LEFT

You don't have any fight left in your marrow,
and there are white flags in your eyes
where your push used to reside.

You lie down,
extinguished.
Your spine melted down into something
that resembles the worst kind of coward.

You don't have what it takes.
You're a runner.

And nothing worth a damn ever
came from bowing out or giving up.

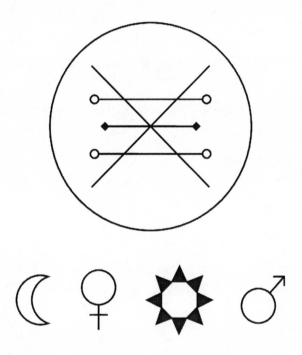

LEARNING TO SPEAK

restarting my oral motor

LEAVING

I stuck two fingers in the ashes of a failed marriage,
and I adorned my forehead, cheeks, lips.

I realized you were a house in which I no longer felt safe.

I buried our remains in the backyard,
packed my suitcase,
fed the dog.

I left.

You had already been gone so long.

The front door was your headstone,
and I left fresh flowers on the welcome mat.

STOP THE LOOP

It's alright if you don't want to be here in my life.
I'm not making an effort to keep you in it
when it's quite clear to me that you're just passing through.

And if you could stop looping back around to take
a little more of me each time,
I think I could heal.

I can't let you use me as a pit stop anymore.
I can't let you come and go as you please.

BEFORE I LEAVE

My skin is crawling, and I hate this place.

Where are my keys?

They won't help me leave, but
they'll feel familiar in my hands.

I'm choking on your scent.

Go away.
Please.

I can't get back to being me
if you linger here like
the ghost I never realized
you had always been.

FLIGHTLESS BIRDS

I desperately wanted to believe
I was lucky to have you for as long as I did.
That's the thing about falling in love
with someone who moves like the wind:
taking flight is inevitable. I loved your feathers.
I was sad to watch you go,
but would have loved you less if you had stayed—
if you had clipped your wings
and become something other than
what I fell for.

POCKET CHANGE

Sometimes I wonder about where you are
and what you are doing when I am not with you.
I wonder more about the other women who come to
visit when I am not the one visiting.
I wonder if we are alike,
if we are several of the same coins
making noise in your pocket as you walk
down the street in your signature white t-shirt
and that hat you've had for far too long.

You reach in and run your fingers over us
before you choose one to play with,
turn us over in your palm,
flip us between your knuckles.
We play along, delighted to be in your presence.
I wonder if the other women miss you
like I do when I'm not the one you pull
so generously from your pocket.
I wonder if they wish, like I do,
that you'd find you don't need the others.
I wonder if they wonder about me
and if we all do our best never to ask
which of us is the lucky coin you'll never get rid of.

FROM SO FAR AWAY

That song about the freckles in our eyes
comes barreling like a subway car
through my headphones and takes me way back.
Late summer, back in college,
riding around in your little green Honda.
The windows were down, and even though
the stars were out, you still had your sunglasses on.
The Postal Service sang through your speakers
about how everything
looks perfect from far away.
Now, years later,
I may even let myself miss you for a moment
or at least miss the way we look
from so far away.

WANTS AND NEEDS

The best thing I ever did
was stop begging you
to stay when all you wanted to do
was go.
It was a dreadfully wonderful thing,
realizing in the midst of wanting you,
that your leaving was what I needed
in order to ignite peace within me.
And these days,
it's easier to discern between
what I want
and
what I need.

RUMORS

I heard you met a girl out west,
I heard she's sorta pretty but not as pretty as me.
But maybe they just saw the tears welling up
in my eyes, and maybe they just wanted to
make me feel better.
I heard California looks good on you,
and you look good in the Pacific.
I heard a lot of things.
For what it's worth,
it sounds like perhaps
you fit there better
than you ever fit me.
And that's alright
because I'm fresh out of
giving a damn.

THE FUNNY THING ABOUT PROMISES

I asked you not to be one of those things
I would have to end up saying goodbye to.
And in a strange way,
I was sort of relieved when you told me
you couldn't promise me that.
Maybe I'll have to say goodbye one day,
but I'll take perfect little unmade promises
today over broken ones tomorrow.

NOWHERE TO PRAY

There is an ancient city burning beneath my skin.
There is smoke trapped in the bottom layers, and you want in.

You can't taste the warnings on my tongue
left behind by those before you.

They would tell you I am a temple in ruins,
but all you want is to have someplace to pray.

I just don't want to be the reason
you call your god a liar.

THE BLUE HAT

On the last morning you kissed me goodbye,
you gave me your blue hat (you said it was teal)
because my hair was a mess and
because it was cold outside.

A keepsake.

I haven't brought myself to wear it
since that morning,
but I can't bring myself
to throw it away either.

I don't even really miss you
like I thought I might when I was
walking away wearing that blue hat.

But I keep it around.
In case my ears get cold.
In case you ask for it back one day.
In case February never ends.

NOT READY

You keep asking me for the truth,
to tell you what you think I'm going to say.
But you're so focused on assumptions,
there is no space for the air in my lungs
to expel such truth, which is eating my insides.
I am not ready for high beams.
I want love more than I ever have,
but now is not the time.
Center stage will have to wait.
I have so much left to do in the shadows
before my curtain comes up.
The spotlight is so warm,
but I am not ready to give up the cold just yet.

PRAYING

Forgetting you is an obscene hope,
a waste of want,
but I have never been frugal
with my pointless prayers.

I press my palms together against
the center of my chest and
begin to mumble something
about a *sorry.*

I shut my eyes,
and in the darkness of the backs
of my eyelids,
your face is starting to fade
like autumn leaves.
And I'm oddly content.

BRUISES

There is a constellation of
translucent bruises stretched across
my shoulder blades, one from each time
you kissed me.

My mind has let go.
It never thinks of you.

My heart, it is busy
mending itself and it told me
to wish you well.

My body—such a
mutinous being—my body will not
forget you.

SELF-SABOTAGE

"People treat you the way you let them," he said.

And that was probably the most painful truth
that ever came charging through my insides.
It settled like black soot in the bottom of my lungs.

The hardest of truths are often the ones
that need to be heard the most.

I held onto his last few words
as I gathered the strength
to let him go.

I don't think either of us
knew he would be
his own demise.

ALARM CLOCK

I no longer dream about being what you want,
no longer want to mold myself into what you need.
I wasn't meant to fit.
I have made peace with that.
I can't be for everyone, love.
I am nothing if I am so universal
that I have no unique parts.
And I have finally awoken to the facts.
Morning finally feels like home.

IN THE MIRROR

That girl in the mirror is going to save me.
She doesn't know it yet.
Her and I spend most days up in arms
with one another, hoping the other will
surrender.
She's a stubborn one,
that girl in the mirror.
Then again, so am I.
But we're getting to know each other again;
we may even be friends one day.
And that's all I can really ask for.

SHE'S GONE

I don't know what version of me you fell in love with.
I know I dislike the one I became beneath your hands—
carrying your heart, sporting a noose.
I don't like that one.
I can promise you
the woman you're looking for
isn't here anymore.

WHITE FLAG

I don't want your sympathy,
your approval,
or even your understanding.

I had wasted too many years
seeking those things,
and when I found I was at
my breaking point,
when I was at the end of my rope
with nowhere to turn
and nothing else to hold onto,
I threw up my white flag
with a pretty little cursive
fuck you
painted across it.

And then I was able to breathe.
And this,
this is living.

DAMAGED GOODS

I am not a pile of shattered glass
meant for your trash can.
I am a goddamn stained glass mosaic.
Look at how my edges glisten
in the sun.
Look at how damaged goods can be
so beautiful.

UNCHAINING ME

The most beautiful sound I've ever heard
was that of my shackles hitting the ground,
echoing through the quiet like a knife
cutting flesh.
Few can understand the weight of things
that seem impossible to change.
I carried those things around like a burden,
a curse,
like something I was ashamed of.
Shame. To feel ashamed.
Shame is the word for the weight.
It's epiphanic—to realize it is more in your power
than you believed to be free of these things,
to have been able to reach the key
to your own unlocking.

LIGHT WITHIN

I've got a belly full of rainbows
wrapped in stone skin,
and I don't remember hearing
any rainfall,
but if you've got the patience
to chip away the rock,
if you can crack me open,
I promise there is a prism reflecting light
within me
that wants to soak you indigo.

THE WILD IN ME

I remember being uncorrupted—
with virgin petals,
untamed and uncut hips,
and thorns intact.
It is the picture of myself
I am working
every day to reclaim.

I have missed the wild in me,
but it's coming home,
it's almost here,
and I've already promised myself
to never let another pluck
my petals and cut
down my thorns,
leaving me barren
and defenseless.

My wild is coming back to me,
and this time
I am ready to own it.

UNCONDITIONAL

I had an entire life before you.

I'm not crisp or brand new,
and I'm far too complex
to fold nicely and neatly into
the front compartment
of your wallet.

My scars shimmer
in the sunlight,
and I have never been
more proud of my
exposed skin.

I promise, if you can
love all of me,
my skeletons will
make room for yours
in my closet, and
I will love them
as I love mine,
as I can love you.

SMALL VICTORIES

Take notice of the first time
you look in the mirror
and it doesn't make you
want to cringe.

Remember the time you tried
on a new outfit and really liked it.

Hold onto the first time
you don't count calories
or pull at your clothes
or stare at the floor
as you walk passed a strange man.

Each of those moments
is a victory.

Your victory.

It only gets easier from there.

LET THE TRUTH COME

We are always at war with the truths
we keep locked inside, which
slowly try to make their way
into the light.
Lay down your sword.
Open the gates.
Let them come.
You will be scarred,
but they will no longer
be crushing your wind pipe.
Breathe.
You're going to be just fine.

THE OCEAN IN ME

There are tectonic plates embedded in the muscles covering my heart,
and as you made your way inside,
they shifted.
An ocean formed at my center,
providing somewhere for you to swim.
You collected coral from my ocean bottom,
something to adorn yourself with.
You made a bed of seaweed,
somewhere for you to rest.
It took me a long time,
but I no longer see the color
of your eyes
in the sea foam
that collects on my shores.
My beach is no longer littered
with your remains.

DEFECTIVE LUNGS

There must be something wrong with my lungs.
You walked into the room,
and I didn't hyperventilate.
You said hello,
and I did not have to catch my breath
before responding.
I think they are broken,
Or maybe they are putting themselves
back together.

PAIN, THE SAVIOR

You kind of have to take the pain
and weave it all together
until it resembles a rope.
Sling it over your shoulder
and just leave it there.
One of these days,
you're going to need it.
It'll be the lifeline that
rescues you from numbness.

THE HOLY FUCK LOVE

I don't care if it comes from a man or woman,
I will settle for nothing less than
a *holy fuck* love.
Please, whoever you are,
come and turn my world sideways
with passion and devotion,
the likes of which I've never
seen nor felt.
Bring me something
to believe in.
I'm waiting.
Come home.

COURAGE

Courage is growing
amidst the daffodil springboard
beneath my feet
and finally,
finally
I am learning how to speak.

LEARNING TO SPEAK

A poetry book
by
Kat Savage

INSTAGRAM: @KAT.SAVAGE

A PRIVATE COMPANY

Elias Joseph Mennealy
Ryan Christopher Lutfalah
Christopher Poindexter

CPSIA information can be obtained
at www.ICGtesting.com
Printed in the USA
FSOW01n0224010216
16396FS